OKS BY MARISSA PIESMAN . . . .

SONAL EFFECTS

RTHODOX PRACTICES

YUPPIE HANDBOOK (with Marilee Hartley)

HEADING U

. . . .

B

P
U
T

MARISSA PIESMAN

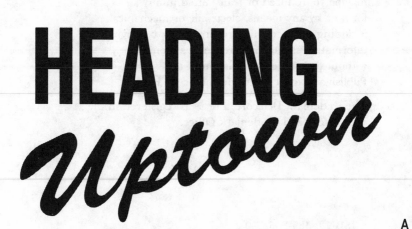

HEADING
Uptown

A
NINA FISCHMAN
MYSTERY

**Delacorte
Press**

Published by
Delacorte Press
Bantam Doubleday Dell Publishing Group, Inc.
666 Fifth Avenue
New York, New York 10103

ISBN 0-385-30537-0

Interior design by Christine Swirnoff

Manufactured in the United States of America

AUTHOR'S NOTE

Many people helped me with ideas and information for this book. These include Lori Brennen, Elaine Budd, Suzanne Cogan, Shawn Coyne, Ellen Count, Brian DeFiore, Mary DiStephan, Jackie Farber, Eleanor Hyde, Ronnie Greenstein Kravitz, Lita Lepie, Diane Ouding, Jane Rosenberg, and Bernice Selden. I am indebted to them all. I am also grateful to my agent, Janet Wilkens Manus, for her guidance and unending enthusiasm, and to my husband, Jeffrey Marks, for his loving support.

HEADING UPTOWN

1 . . . .

Funerals brought out the best in her mother, Nina thought,
as Ida narrated their way through Queens. Nina and Ida
Fischman were on the 8:32 to Great Neck, en route to Helen
Hirsch's funeral. Ida was going on and on. She had a ten-
dency not only to meander but also to verge on the nostalgic.
Which was hopeless when it came to activities requiring crisp
optimism, like picking stocks, but just perfect for all death-
related activities.

Nina's mother was great at visiting terminally ill patients,
comforting bereaved relatives, and warming you up for the
funeral of someone you hadn't seen in quite some time. Ida
was a natural historian who knew how to throw in enough
fiction to keep up the dramatic tension. And she was replete
with details, like a big fat colorful nineteenth-century novel,
inching forward slowly. Not like those anemic postmodern
books people turned out these days, written in black and
white. Ida's narrative line, like her waistline, was ample.

And like those Victorian novelists that got paid by the

word, Ida's stories let you tune in and out without missing any important plot developments. Right now Nina had taken the opportunity to fix her attention on Shea Stadium, outside the grimy train window, since Ida seemed to have gone off on a tangential subplot involving the deceased's sister-in-law.

"I hope you're taking this all in," Ida snapped. Like any good narrator, she could tell when she was losing her audience. "Don't forget that you're the executor of Helen's will."

The streets of Flushing blurred as Ida's words came sharply into focus. "Holy shit," Nina said.

"You forgot, didn't you?"

"Well, it was a long time ago." Nina remembered now. Helen Hirsch was a college friend of her mother. Helen and Ida had been Hunter girls, back in the thirties, when the smart sons of immigrant families went to City College and the smart daughters mostly went to work. Except for the persistent ones who somehow managed to talk their bewildered parents into letting them go to Hunter. Which meant a year of mandatory Latin and a chance for you to meet young women from German Jewish families who lived on West End or Park Avenue. These women would invite you to their homes occasionally and you would be in awe of the crystal and china and the impeccable English of their parents, who had subscriptions to the opera and the Philharmonic. And then you would go back to the Bronx and be filled with impatience at the Yiddish accents and the Yahrzeit glasses that served as the Baccarat of the boroughs.

Helen and Ida had lived through this together and this mutual coming-of-age had served to forge a bond that had remained unbroken. When her mother got together with her friend, Nina was always amazed at the changes that came over the two of them. They seemed to bestow upon each other the rosy romantic expectations of prewar New York City. Varicose veins would deswell, osteoporosis would re-